Peace on Purpose

God's Wisdom for Calming the Chaos in Life

Jennifer Stengel-Mohr

www.rdtalleybooks.com

Plainsboro, New Jersey

The primary Bible version referenced in this book is the New King James Version. Scriptures from other versions are noted next to the scripture.

Cover Designed by Michela Fellows

ISBN: 978-1-7342540-3-7

Copyright © 2020 by Jennifer Stengel-Mohr

All rights reserved. No part of this publication may be reproduced, distributed, or transmitted in any form or by any means, including photocopying, recording, or other electronic or mechanical methods without the prior written permission of the publisher. For permission requests, solicit the publisher via the address or website below.

R.D. Talley Books Publishing
P.O. Box 45
Plainsboro, New Jersey 08536
www.rdtalleybooks.com

Dedication

To my Father in Heaven who fills me with His words and to my father on earth, who is now in heaven, thank you for setting my feet on the path to Jesus.

Thank you to my mother for your love and support.

I also want to thank all my family and friends who walk with me on this journey, especially my husband Bill and my wonderful son, Billy. You are all a blessing to me.

Preface

"Not that I have already attained, or am already perfected; but I press on, that I may lay hold of that for which Christ Jesus has also laid hold of me. ¹³ Brethren, I do not count myself to have apprehended; but one thing I do, forgetting those things which are behind and reaching forward to those things which are ahead, ¹⁴ I press toward the goal for the prize of the upward call of God in Christ Jesus."

Philippians 3:12-14

Paul spoke these words in Philippians while he was on his mission to establish the early church. He was under tremendous pressure and persecution from all sides. Paul understood that we are all a work-in-progress which will come to completion when we enter the Kingdom of God. Knowing we will never meet perfection here in this life should give us a different perspective on how we should behave while on earth. Our gaze should be focused upward as we strive to reach that ultimate place of peace in Heaven.

One thing is for sure: in order to pursue this and find true peace, we need to be all-in. There is no room for compromise. We cannot hold onto earthly ideals while reaching for Heaven's glory.

God has placed the content of this book on my heart but I, in no way, claim to have taken full hold of it all personally. I am still on the journey of pressing toward the goal of living more like Christ each day.

As with most books, it can be several years in the making before it is published. I was working on this final version during the unprecedented time of the world-wide Coronavirus Pandemic. Even in these seemingly dark times, God still shines His light through people. If we open our hearts to God, he will illuminate all the dark areas in our lives. I pray that God will meet you where you are in your spiritual journey and allow these insights to touch your heart, mind and spirit, in Jesus' name.

Table of Contents

Introduction 9

Finding Peace Through Creativity
Who Are We Created To Be? 14

Finding Peace Through Communication
How Do Our Words Influence Our Lives &
The Lives Of Others? 25

Finding Peace In Relationships
How Can We Foster Healthy Relationships? 38

Finding Peace of Mind
Who Is Influencing Our Mind? 52

Finding Peace Within Our Body
How Can We Get Our Body To Function
At Optimal Levels? 62

Finding Peace Within Our Spirit
What Does Our Spirit Need To Grow? 72

Finding Peace For Provision
Who Is Our Provider? 80

Finding Peace Over Timing
Whose Timing Is It Anyway? 88

Finding Peace through Forgiveness
We All Need Forgiveness, So How Do We Forgive?........... 94
Closing Thoughts... 100
Appendix 103

Introduction

"These things I have spoken to you, that in Me you may have peace. In the world you will have tribulation; but be of good cheer, I have overcome the world."

John 16:33

Every experience in life, whether good or bad, provides an opportunity for growth. These experiences become our testimony or story. God is the author of that story. Imagine reading a book with only one character in it. It probably wouldn't be a very good read. We cannot create our story alone. God sent Jesus into our journey so we could have a glorious adventure on our way to Heaven.

Because Jesus lived as a man on earth, there is no experience we can have that He would not understand. He knows we will encounter trouble here on earth, but He left us His Spirit and The Word (Holy Bible). Both of these things are a direct conduit to God and His supernatural power. The reason Jesus endured and had peace in suffering was because He intimately possessed both the Spirit and the Word of God. Even until death, He chose to focus on God and God's will. Peace is a choice.

Choice is only authentic when the person who is making it is informed. I have chosen to believe in Jesus, not because someone has told me to, but because I have seen Him working through my life and in the lives of others. Once you have experienced a relationship with Jesus, it is very difficult to deny that He exists.

One thing that particularly troubles me in these times is what I call, Compliant Christianity. I apply this in situations when someone goes through the motions of thought, word or deed out of a perceived obligation to God. One example may be attending church on special holidays or maybe every Sunday, but not living by example the rest of the year. Another example is rote repetition of prayer without any meaning behind it. These examples are dangerous because they are misleading. One might think that these actions are pleasing to God because they simply "showed up". However, this does not produce the type of relationship that God is seeking with us.

My concern is that these misleading assumptions are perpetuated by the history of the modern (and sometimes traditional) church environment. Many modern church teachings glance over, or completely leave out the aspect of a true relationship with God through Jesus. Emphasis is often placed on religion, traditions and doctrine over intimacy and true supernatural power from the Holy Spirit. We are warned about such practices in Revelation, and told not to be lukewarm (Revelation 3:14-22). God lives outside the walls of the church building and inside of us. Reading God's Word and connecting with Him daily will reveal truth, so we can make an informed choice. Once we make the choice to accept Him, our entire life changes.

The human condition is the natural equalizer. Everyone, without exception, will succumb to our human state. However, what differs is how our journey will look while we are here, and what we are setting ourselves up for beyond this life. We must position ourselves with the correct mindset and develop the resources we need to build the best life. This is not to say that there will not be challenges. Those are to be expected. Remarkably, this is another equalizer. At some point we will all face challenges. Our challenges may look different based on our circumstances, but they can all be traced back to one of the fundamental aspects of the human condition. So, what determines the success of how we emerge from the challenges in this journey we call life? It's simple: choice!

The choices we make at each crossroad will determine the outcome, not only in our life, but in the lives around us. Understanding this fact begins with the knowledge that we have been given the ability to have choice in the first place. God created and gifted us with free will. Ultimately, this is so we can choose to have a relationship with Him. However, this principle applies to every other aspect of our lives as well. While we may not choose the circumstances that we find ourselves in, we do have a choice about how we deal with them.

Knowing how to properly deal with our circumstances and having the ability to make rightful choices comes from an intimacy with the one who created us and the world we live in. Choosing Jesus to be our partner in this journey will make all the difference. Not to trivialize this by any means, but rather as a way to illustrate its significance, I will use the following example. Suppose you are playing a new board game. Would you not first sit down and read the rules made by the creator of the game? This would give you maximum advantage to emerge as the winner. God created this world and gives us the rules for how to navigate it through His Word. We are foolish if we do not read the instructions laid-out by Him.

We are all on the same journey of life yet taking different paths. What is going to matter in the end is who was on that journey with us. Accepting Jesus is a choice, but the alternative causes unnecessary struggle and strife which ultimately leads to a dead-end, both physically and spiritually.

The revelations in this book come from daily scripture reading and meditation along with prayer and my personal testimony of how God revealed himself in my life. God's Word is enough! The insights in this book are meant to encourage you in your daily application and practical use of the scriptures. Each chapter addresses one element of the human experience and how to strive for peace in that area. There are several tools built into each chapter to help you along your journey to discovering peace.

- A **Focus Scripture** is included for meditation.
- The **Key Insight** is a guiding statement to reflect upon during the reading and beyond.
- The **Affirmation** is a positive thought or word focus for daily encouragement.

- A **Relevant Quote** is provided for inspiration (sometimes it is helpful to post these quotes in a visible location while we are working through a situation)
- **Reflection Questions** and **Action Steps** can be found at the end of every chapter to use as a follow-up.

These tools serve as a way to continue the application of The Word in daily life. While the chapters are independent of one another, they are interrelated due to the nature of the content. Feel free to set your own pace for reading. The book's format accommodates either a sequential or self-selected method of reading.

It is my sincere prayer that seeing God's perspective, which is given to us by His Word, will help you in your decision-making on a daily basis. Once you say, *Yes*, God will open-up paths that you never knew existed. Paths which lead to joy, abundance and peace.

Finding Peace Through Creativity

"In the beginning God created the heavens and the earth."

Genesis 1:1

Key Insight: Creation is revelation, revelation begins transformation, transformation brings peace.

Affirmation: I have a unique identity in Christ and I will share my authentic gifts wherever God leads me.

In book one, chapter one, verse one of The Bible, God establishes himself as The Creator. Since God began here, it seemed logical to put creativity as chapter one. God is the master artist with the universe as a canvas. He carefully selected each detail to dot his landscape. If we read further in Genesis 1:27, we discover that we were created in God's image, therefore we also have the ability to create. Why is this important to the human condition? When we create, our spirit is in alignment with God's Spirit and this brings revelation. Through revelation we experience transformation.

I want to establish that, as I mention creativity in this chapter, I am not just addressing it in terms of artistic creativity. Artistic endeavors are extremely valuable and promoted by God. However, I would like to broaden the definition of creativity to include any instance when humans have the capability to manifest a novel idea, or object, into being in order to create something that did not previously exist.

Now that we have expanded our definition of creativity, let's reconsider what it means to have choice. Typically, we might consider choice as a binary option; it's either this or that. However, combining choice with creativity can allow us the option of creating infinite new possibilities. Alignment with the Spirit of God gives us supernatural insights that can help us develop solutions to challenging problems. Remember, God created the world and everything in it, then left it to us to steward it. This means that within us is the capability to address the world's earthly needs by God's supernatural power that flows through us. We have all been gifted with different skills and talents. Understanding how to use these abilities creatively to serve others is where we find our purpose. What matters in the end is what we did for others, not for ourselves.

When we are centered in Christ, we receive inspired creativity. This form of creativity reveals to us our uniqueness and begins to outline our true purpose in life. I call this our authentic gifts. Our authentic gifts are the things that God wants us to contribute to the world; things the world needs that only we can provide. We are God's hands and feet and He has created us to do His Will here on earth. The use of our creative energy should always honor God and bless others.

God created our DNA. Deoxyribonucleic Acid is the scientific matter that makes us who we are. It is the tiny molecules that make us completely unique. As Ephesians 2:10 (KJV) tells us, "For we are His workmanship, created in Christ Jesus unto good works, which God hath before ordained that we should walk in them." God's intention is for us to be unique. We were created by Him for a unique purpose. Let's imagine for a moment that DNA stands for *Do Not Assimilate*. If we are meant to be unique, then why do we always try to conform?

When Jesus was on this earth, he did not assimilate. His mission was to challenge the status quo, to set apart God's people and draw them to Him. Jesus knew who He was and followed who God designed Him to be up until His last breath. We can say He was perfect because He lived-out His exact purpose in life. We need to stop trying so hard to define who we are based on what others believe or who society tells us we should be. The Creator has made us His own. We need to discover who God wants us to be and what good works He wants us to accomplish. Be the 'you' that God intended for you to be and you will find peace.

From an early age we are bombarded with the question, "What do you want to be when you grow up?" Our entire childhood is a primer for getting to this ultimate place of being something or someone of value to others. In that process of discovery, are we looking toward what God has planned for us? Do we understand our identity in Him? Ultimately, what we do when we grow up should align to what God is calling us to do.

Consider this: When you meet someone new, how do you introduce yourself? Do you say your name and then tell what you do? This is very common but our identity should not be tied to a job title or our relationship to someone else. Being a doctor, teacher, mother or wife is NOT WHO WE ARE. Those are just roles that have been given to us, or those that we have willingly accepted. We need to understand that we already have an identity in Christ. We are a REDEEMED CHILD OF THE KING. Once we understand that, then we can begin to live-out what God has planned for us.

What you are is God's gift to you.
What you become is your gift to God.
- Danish Proverb

We begin to see a bit of our purpose when we look at what we do in the roles we have been given. How does The Spirit move us when we are working? Are we a caregiver, leader, problem solver? Those inner workings are part of our identity and purpose that God has for us, no matter where we end up serving.

Earnestly seeking creativity through a spiritual connection with God is what starts to transform us. This connection also reveals to us our identity and God-given purpose. We discover how to contribute positively to the world that God has placed us in. When we live-out our higher sense of purpose and the true identity we are called to, we experience peace.

Since God is a creator, He does not make carbon copies. Everything he makes is authentic and unique. We are authentic and unique! We simply cannot be someone other than who God made us to be and expect to find peace. An intimate relationship with God will transform us into our true self. Jesus never lost sight of His true self and His bigger purpose. Worldly distractions did not take Him off-course because He was completely aligned with God's Spirit and knew who He was.

The earth is ruled and influenced by Satan (2 Corinthians 4:4). Society often reflects this fact with twisted lies and counterfeit identities. When Jesus was tempted in the wilderness, Satan told Him all sorts of lies. Satan feared the power that Jesus had because God's spirit lived inside Him. That same Spirit lives inside us and we often fail to abide by it. Satan does everything in his power to separate us from the purpose God intended for our lives.

Satan is fully aware of the power we would have if we truly lived-out our God-given purpose. Just like Jesus, we would be laser focused and unstoppable in accomplishing what God has set before us. We have believed Satan's lies for too long and need to realign our spirit to God's Spirit. We can accomplish this when we know the truth.

The beautiful thing about our true identity and authentic gifts is that God never forgets them. We may lose sight of our true selves from time to time, but God will never abandon who he made us to be. He will put us in situations and relationships that allow us to demonstrate our true identity.

When I was fourteen years old, I made my confirmation in the Lutheran Church. This was a joyous time for me because it was a passage into young adulthood and a chance to choose how I wanted to worship. I became a Sunday School teacher and quickly realized that teaching was something that suited me. By the time I turned eighteen years old, I was leading the Sunday School Program at my church. I was about to graduate high school and I sensed that I should go into ministry. I started to search for programs to attend for college and began to get excited about my decision.

Then I started to talk with others about my decision and the excitement slowly faded. Everyone, including my parents, shared with me the fact that this might not be a practical decision. All the typical objections came into the mix: How will you find a position? Will you make enough money? Isn't that going to be a difficult life? Do they allow women in ministry? Slowly, I talked myself out of this option.

I decided to enroll in the local liberal arts university since I was now unsure of where I would end up. I took a 100-level linguistics course as a requirement and was intrigued with all aspects of language. It was exciting and I was excelling in it, so I decided to make it my major. It is ironic because I did not even know that linguistics was an area of study until I had taken that course.

More than halfway through my new major, I actually discovered that using linguistics to make a living was not really attainable. Once again, I found myself bombarded with all the questions I had been asked only a few years earlier. I was advised to add education courses to my major, so when I finished my degree I could teach. That sounded logical since I did well with teaching at the church.

Fast forward, I am still an educator until this day, more than 25 years later. However, God did not forget the true identity that he had for me, which he showed me while I was a teen. I was to teach and minister His Word. When I came to the realization that I needed to pursue ministry again, it occurred to me that God had provided me with various opportunities throughout those years to do small versions of this along the way.

I taught Vacation Bible School at my church, conducted women's retreats and ministered to friends and family. I discovered that no matter what role I found myself in, I was always teaching and ministering to someone. My authentic gifts to teach and minister were always in the forefront of the work I did regardless of the environment I found myself in. This gave me confidence to move forward in ministry because I now had more than two decades of professional education experience and knew how to reach people with His message. So, although years had passed, I was back on the same road I had glanced down when I was 18. I was there because God did not forget!

As I began my journey towards ministry, I started to pursue writing and speaking for Christ. During a conversation with someone about my new pursuits she said to me, "Oh cool! Maybe you will be the next…" You can fill in the blank with a famous person's name. I replied, "No, I am going to be Jen Mohr, the one and only." The woman did not know what to say, literally. I guess she wasn't expecting me to be original.

We have become so accustomed to just filling in blanks or fitting in boxes that we have lost our authenticity and originality. I call this the Cubicle Effect. You are familiar with an office cubicle, this tiny space with walls that form a boundary we should not pass. This physical space impacts our mental state as well. It limits creativity, originality and doesn't allow us to think outside the box. Satan wants to keep us in a box so we become unaware of the limitless potential that God has instilled in us through the Holy Spirit. God lives outside the box. He calls us to be set-apart and different.

In the current day, this mindset is partly fueled by social media, which inadvertently exploits us and makes us believe that we are in the spotlight every day and need to perform as someone other than ourselves. Satan has been busy creating distractions, luring us to sin and whispering comparisons in our ear, while slowly distancing us from who God has called us to be. If we are truly unique, which we are, then we cannot compare ourselves to others in our journey.

My primary concern is particularly for young girls today. Young ladies are growing up in a time when images of what it means to be a woman are very distorted. There is a tension caused between two extremes. On one hand, women are portrayed as sexual icons with the sole purpose of being submissive to a man. On the other hand, women are portrayed as warriors, who are to be stronger and smarter than men.

Here is the problem with both extremes: they leave out the true identity of a woman. Women do not gain power by measuring themselves against others, they gain power when they are connected to God. God cannot bless us when we are pretending to be someone else. Transforming to become who God intended us to be is powerful. We should embrace with open arms the life that God is leading us to because this is going to be the most fruitful and peaceful path we can take.

So, reflecting back on my authentic gifts and identity for ministry, I can recall a small detail with great significance. From as early as I can remember, I regularly received journals as gifts for various occasions.

While I truly appreciated and liked every one of them, most of them were never really utilized. I wondered what it was about me that prompted others to think a journal would make a fitting gift.

      Years later, when I moved into my new home, I unpacked a box of blank journals and realized that it was a tool I should have been using all along to record the thoughts that God had been conveying to me. Now as I write this book, I am flipping through the filled pages of over a year's worth of conversations with the Lord. God knew I would need those journals as I began to move into my true purpose of sharing His Word with others. When I look back at these notes, there are new revelations each time as God begins to paint a picture with His Words. When God sets your feet on His Path, He will be sure to cover all the details. Find peace knowing God will walk with you as you transform into your true identity.

Reflection:

What skills, talents and gifts have you been blessed with?

How can you use these to serve?

What is God calling you to do that is uniquely set out for you and no one else?

Action Steps:

- Spend some quiet time with God and ask him to reveal to you something about yourself.
- Journal or sketch what he is showing you.
- Get creative. Make a vision board (collage) for your unique identity and/or authentic gifts. (See instructions in the Appendix)

Finding Peace Through Communication

"When you enter a house, first say, 'Peace to this house.' ⁶ If someone who promotes peace is there, your peace will rest on them; if not, it will return to you."

Luke 10:5-6, NIV

Key Insight: Peace begins with us…and our words.

Affirmation: I will speak words that are life affirming and bring peace into every situation that I encounter.

Language follows the law of attraction. Like magnets, words can attract or repel with great force. Every word we speak matters. Our words become the manifestation of our lives. Multiple verses in scripture bring awareness to the power of our words. We are told that life and death are in the power of the tongue (Proverbs 18:21). This is not just physical life and death, but spiritual life and death as well. Furthermore, Matthew 12:37 says, "For by your words you will be justified, and by your words you will be condemned." These verses make it clear that our outcomes are determined by our words. This can either become something positive or negative depending on the which words we choose.

All of creation started with a word. In Genesis 1:3, God said, "let there be light." All of existence was called into being by the Word of God. John 1:1 tells us, "In the beginning was the Word, and the Word was with God and the Word was God." Satan knew early-on the power that the Word can possess. Therefore, since the beginning of time he has been distorting and manipulating language to lure people away from God. In Genesis 3:1, the serpent asks Eve, "Did God say you shall not eat from any tree in the garden?" This example demonstrates that manipulation and deception through the use of language is as old as our existence. Satan was tempting Eve by twisting God's words. We should be on alert and be discerning of all that we hear and all that we say.

Can we be identified as one of the followers of Jesus by the way we speak? That is exactly what is being revealed in Matthew 26:73, "And a little later those who stood by came up and said to Peter, "Surely you also are *one* of them, for your speech betrays you." In this verse, Jesus had just been arrested and Peter was being asked if he knows Him. We know that Peter denies Jesus three times, but his speech gives him away. Because he sounds like Jesus, Peter is accused of knowing Him. Are we so intimate with Jesus that His words are our words? We must examine everything that comes from our lips and verify that it aligns with The Word of God. We must speak truth, beauty, wisdom, righteousness and most of all, love.

Paul tells us in Philippians 4:8 (NIV), "Finally, brothers and sisters, whatever is true, whatever is noble, whatever is right, whatever is pure, whatever is lovely, whatever is admirable—if anything is excellent or praiseworthy—think about such things." And these are the things we should also speak about, meaning we must remove negativity, hate, defeat, uncleanliness and profanity from our vocabulary.

Again, Paul tells us in 1 Peter 3:10-11, "He who would love life and see good days, let him refrain his tongue from evil, and his lips from speaking deceit.[11] Let him turn away from evil and do good; Let him seek peace and pursue it." Here we are shown again that a good life is determined by our tongue and how we speak. We need to guard our words in order to bring about peace in our lives.

I have been trained as a linguist and have worked in the field of language education for nearly 25 years. Understanding how language works is not only my profession, but a passion of mine since as early as I can remember. For a very long time I compartmentalized my understanding of how humans use language and how God intends for us to use language. One morning, several months back, God spoke to me clearly in the spirit and revealed to me that all of my professional training in this area was in order to communicate an understanding to others about how important our words are, both as individuals and as a society.

The principles discussed in this chapter are evidenced by linguistic theory, current events and undoubtably, scripture. It is my sincere belief that if followers of Christ reclaim the jurisdiction over language, worldly issues will begin to fall back into place and we will see more peace. This is possible because language influences how we think, and how we think impacts our language use.

In my role as a linguistics professor, I have analyzed language for over two decades. It is a fascinating topic of study and quite relevant to many aspects of life. The current climate within society and politics reflect just how powerful language can be. Many subgroups within these environments are keenly aware of this power and have used it to manipulate their agendas. If you can change the language, you can change the way people think. My intention here is not to turn this chapter into a political stance, but rather to illustrate how easily deceptive this practice can become.

So, how do you turn fiction into the truth so that others believe it? Simply manipulate the language associated with it. Satan knew this back in the Garden of Eden. I will provide a few examples here to give context to this concept.

Linguistically speaking, the prefix, *pro-*, appears before a word to indicate a favorable relationship with the word to follow. For example, *pro-war*. When debating two sides of an issue, the different viewpoints look at opposite angles of the same issue. You can either be *for* or *against* something, but you cannot be both. Therefore, using the same example, the opposite side of this debate would be *anti*-war or *pro*-peace. To show opposition, you either use the negative prefix, *anti-* meaning against, or you take on the opposite word of the argument and add *pro-* to it. In this case the opposite of war is peace.

Now let's apply this linguistic theory to the issue of abortion. In this debate, one is either labeled *pro-life* or *pro-choice.* These are not opposite sides of the same issue. *Choice* is not the opposite of *Life.* If you are not *for life*, then you are *for death*. However, the movement would not gain any followers if their platform was labeled *pro-death* or *anti-life*. The manipulation of the language helps soften the debate about abortion. Who could argue with being *pro-choice*, right? That sounds like a valid viewpoint since we all desire choice.

Selective word choice helps people to overlook the fact that innocent babies are being killed in exchange for empowering women in some sort of twisted murder plot. Words can speak life or death. Remember Proverbs 18:21 (NIV), "The tongue has the power of life and death, and those who love it will eat its fruit." In this case, words are literally a death sentence for unborn children. We can choose to be politically correct or biblically correct in our communication. Both of these choices have consequences.

God has revealed to me some recent patterns of language-use as it relates to spiritual matters. It is obvious that we should abstain from cursing and profanity, but let's be aware of something more subtle in our communication. We have given way to self-censorship, the omission of God from our everyday speech. Due to pressures in society to become politically correct, we have successfully seen the removal of God from all things.

This includes cutting God out of our general speech. We have reduced, "God bless you" to "bless you"; "Christmas" to "xmas". Depending on the company we are in we may abstain from saying "Praise God" or "Thank God". This removal of God from our words begins to remove Him from our minds. The absence of God in our everyday speech is a supposed choice with the intention of not offending others who are non-believers. Yet, within this choice, we are creating an even bigger offense to our God. Our omission in speech is the same as a denial of The Most-High.

Many believers have slowly allowed this mode of thinking to erode their communication and curb their speech. We need to reverse this pattern by standing firm and boldly, proclaiming God's name in public. I am not, by no means, suggesting that we harass or barrage others with righteous words. However, we should not shrink back in fear over the use of God's name either. Acts 4:29 (NIV) proclaims, "Now, Lord, consider their threats and enable your servants to speak your word with great boldness." We are being called to stand up for God. That starts with professing His name and giving Him public honor and glory. We should not censor ourselves, nor allow others to censor God from any and all places.

Satan is very patient and knows that he can lure more people from God using the slow, slippery slope method. If Satan was blatant and honest, we might not be as quick to follow his schemes. However, Satan likes to start small and gradually build-up deception until we are so blinded that we cannot see the damage he has actually caused. He has been particularly crafty in the area of language manipulation.

We see in history a slow removal of God's name, His existence and His Word from every place in society. He has been taken out of schools, media, homes and even some churches. In the 1800's, the first dictionary published by Noah Webster used scripture to define the meaning of everyday words. Now, Webster's dictionary, owned by a multi-billion dollar publishing company, has obviously removed scripture and has also changed the meanings of many words to fit society's ideologies. Some of the recently altered words are *literally, gender* and *racism*.

It is a fact that language changes. Language grows and transforms as people use it. However, research shows that this change tends to be organic and starts from the users of the language and then filters into society as a whole. One pattern of linguistic observation I have noted is the fact that these language changes are now occurring from the top-down.

Influencers, political figures and various figures of the film and entertainment industry grab hold of a meaning of a word that they want to espouse and then infiltrate all aspects of life with this word so that others begin to use it. This is not organic; this is indoctrination. If someone is to speak against their definition of the word using facts or truth, they are at best ignored, if not publicly shamed or ridiculed. Colossians 2:4 warns us of this: "Now this I say lest anyone should deceive you with persuasive words." Paul is speaking to the people of the early church and warning them about deception through the clever use of words. We need to be on guard and watch how words are influencing our thoughts and our lives.

How do we know what is true? Look at the fruit that the words bear. If the platform of speech results in oppression, riots, discord, hate or lawlessness, then that is not truth. Truth will liberate, encourage, spread love and be productive. Choosing our words carefully sets the tone for our life. More importantly, it also impacts everyone around us. If we speak negativity, we will consume negativity. If we speak darkness, we will consume darkness. Yet, if we speak light, we will consume light. If we speak positivity, we will consume positivity. Again, this comes down to the original conversation of choice. We choose our words, therefore, we choose our bounty in life. This implores us to make the choice to speak God's Word whenever we can. If we do, we are sure to attract what is good, what is righteous and what is pure.

Our words align our thoughts and our actions. Words represent our fundamental perspective on life and are a demonstration of what we truly value. We should be mindful of the overuse of reserved words for common everyday purpose. One example is the word *love*. God is love, yet we can also love our shoes. Overuse of important words can begin to muddy their meaning and lessen their power. Humans throw around the word *love* so much. Does it really even hold its true meaning anymore? God's example of love was to send his only son to save us (John 3:16). Do we possess a definition of love that is this strong? I am sure most of us would not literally die for a pair of shoes we love.

Another example is the word *awesome*. It means to inspire awe. God is truly awesome. Who else could create the entire world from nothing and maintain it continually? We should be in awe of God. In awe of a famous celebrity...probably not as much.

OMG..., I almost forgot! I have witnessed countless believers and non-believers alike throw out the Lord's name in all sorts of circumstances. I hear shouts of "Oh My God!", or "Jesus Christ!" daily and it is not for the purpose of praise. It perplexes me how we can trivialize His name in one instance using it totally inappropriately, and then, as I mentioned before, at times when it really matters, we take His name out of our dialogues. God's name and His Word should never be altered, sanitized or polluted.

People may hear your words, but they feel your attitude.
- John C. Maxwell

Teenage years can be difficult for everyone. When we are the teenager, we do not realize how difficult those years are for the people around us. I was a very respectful, diligent and trustworthy teenager by comparison, but no one is perfect. Sure, I made many mistakes. One of the most difficult things during this time was communication with my father. Although we loved each other greatly, it was very difficult for us to talk without ending up in an argument. This was partially due to our similarities in personality and our passion for precision.

On one particular occasion, he was pestering me about something insignificant and with my indignant teenage attitude, I told him to "leave me alone and get a life." He was so personally offended by my remarks that this conversation began the divide in our relationship. Things were not great in our relationship after this point. Difficulty in communicating and a difference in viewpoints drove a wedge in our relationship. There was a time that we did not speak for several years. As time passed, we mended our relationship, but it was not until many years later that I fully realized the impact of my words.

My father was suffering from brain cancer and he knew his time was limited. We were caring for him at home, so we were together a lot. While he was still well enough, we shared lots of memories and talked through some of our past hurts. By this time, my father and I had become quite close. We were at a place where we could be open and honest without hurting one another's feelings. On a particular day near the end of his life, he asked me, "Do you remember when you told me to get a life?" I had a recollection of that conversation, but at the time it was just something teenagers would say and it didn't mean much. Well, for my father it did mean something. He carried that conversation with him all those years and was very hurt by it. Him mentioning it at this particular time illustrated just how much those words impacted him. I began to cry and I sincerely apologized for causing him such pain from my careless choice of words. I simply had no idea how much damage that one phrase had caused. We completely reconciled all things and by the time of his passing, both he and I were at peace with our relationship.

Every word matters and we should filter ourselves before we speak. Now, I know this is much easier said than done. The only way to truly master this is to develop the habit of only speaking life. Once we practice this over and over again, our old words will fall away. There is a saying in the field of linguistics, *"If you do not use it, you lose it."* This is the one time we actually want to have a loss for words. So, to find peace in life, we must strip away all of our words that harm, demean, blaspheme, lie, insult, or cause death to others.

Imagine if the last words we said would be how we were remembered when we move on from this life. What would our words say about us and our life? Would we be remembered as salt and light? Colossians 4:5-6 (NIV) says, "Be wise in the way you act toward outsiders; make the most of every opportunity. [6] Let your conversation be always full of grace, seasoned with salt, so that you may know how to answer everyone."

Most importantly our words should speak love. Positive, life affirming words can transform hearts and minds. If every single person practiced this regularly, imagine the transformation that could take place. The domino effect that it could create would be inspiring. Each person speaking with love and kindness to the next. This would surely bring in believers to the Kingdom when others could witness the fruits of our sweet words. Unfortunately, the opposite is also true. Constant negativity and degrading words can produce a cycle of anger and resentment. This too can become contagious and infectious. So, which option would we rather perpetuate? Love is the language of God. Let us learn to speak it fluently.

In conclusion, praise brings peace. We need to let our praise speak louder than our problems. Praising God, no matter what the circumstances are, replaces our words with His glory. This is a great way to undo a habit of speaking negatively. If we just exchange our words for words of praise, we will watch peace unfold before us and within us.

Reflection:

Was there ever a time that you said something that you wish you could take back?

Do your responses to everyday situations tend to be negative or positive?

Who can you bless with positive words?

Action Steps:

- Be mindful of our tongue and choose our words carefully.
- Strive for positive interactions and speaking life into others.
- Try a new greeting. Instead of hello or good-bye, practice saying "Peace be with you", like Jesus did or "Have a blessed day".
- Bring God back into our daily conversations. Don't censor our spiritual words.

Finding Peace In Relationships

"If someone says, "I love God," and hates his brother, he is a liar; for he who does not love his brother whom he has seen, how can he love God whom he has not seen?"

1 John 4:20

Key Insight: Treat others with love. Everyone is essential and everyone has a purpose.

Affirmation: I will engage others with compassion, integrity and love.

No matter how hard you search, you will never find another relationship that is stronger or more loving than the relationship that is available with God through Jesus Christ. Love is the strongest force in the universe. What more love can there be than to give up your only son to save the world (John 3:16)? God desires an intimate and personal relationship with each person. When we have this true relationship with God, it allows for all of our earthly relationships to have more meaning and become more peaceful. If we want peace in our life, we must find peace in all of our daily relationships.

Jesus is very clear in Matthew 22 verses 37-40 (NIV) that if we are to have good relationships, we must love God first. Jesus replied: "Love the Lord your God with all your heart and with all your soul and with all your mind. ³⁸ This is the first and greatest commandment. ³⁹ And the second is like it: 'Love your neighbor as yourself.' ⁴⁰ All the Law and the Prophets hang on these two commandments." Without acknowledging God first, all other relationships will be a miss.

Our best investment in life is to pour into other people. Every interaction in life is an opportunity to connect with another one of God's creations. Each person that comes along our path is divinely appointed to be there. Now, I know there may be some people who might seem like a distraction or nuisance at times, but believe they are assigned to you for a purpose. When we acknowledge this aspect about our interactions, we can gain perspective and perhaps respect for the people God has placed around us.

Additionally, two characteristics that we learn from Jesus' interactions throughout the Bible are compassion and integrity. Sadly, we might find these lacking from many of the individuals we encounter daily. Compassion is the genuine care for others that moves us to reflect the light of Jesus. Integrity means doing what is right, not what is easy. We cannot go through life with peace if we are not exercising compassion and integrity towards others. The difficulty of this arises in circumstances when we are not shown these things in return. Jesus tells us in Matthew

5:38-40 (NIV), "You have heard that it was said, 'Eye for eye, and tooth for tooth.' ³⁹ But I tell you, do not resist an evil person. If anyone slaps you on the right cheek, turn to them the other cheek also. ⁴⁰ And if anyone wants to sue you and take your shirt, hand over your coat as well." We should always act with compassion and integrity because that is God's Will, not because we are expecting to be treated that way in return.

It is said that people come into our life for a reason or a season. This not only means that there is a reason you are connected to each person around you, but it also means that the time may come when they are no longer part of that circle. Part of having healthy relationships is knowing when it may be time to break ties with someone. If God reveals to us that we should begin to distance ourselves from someone who we currently interact it, it is wise to listen to His leading.

This is particularly difficult if this person is a family member. Sharing a family history with another person does not automatically mean you need to have a close relationship with that person. While we should love everyone, as we are called to do, that doesn't mean they need to be part of our inner circle. In fact, you MUST keep certain people at a distance in order for God to elevate you, help you advance, and bring you peace.

> *Never misuse the one who likes you. Never say busy to the one who needs you. Never cheat on the one who trusts you. Never forget the one who always remembers you.*
>
> *-Unknown*

God has ordained certain relationships in our lives and gives us specific instructions on how to handle such relationships. God's Word regarding relationships is sure to bring us healthy relationships that foster peace. The difficult part to this could be that not both parties are acting according to God's Will where the relationship is concerned. I encourage you to still act with compassion, integrity and love towards them. God can change their heart when we are moving in the Spirit of God. Ephesians 4:2-3 (NIV) says, "Be completely humble and gentle; be patient, bearing with one another in love. Make every effort to keep the unity of the Spirit through the bond of peace." Often, we are quick to dismiss a relationship when we feel it is not going the way we imagined. These verses from Ephesians remind us to bear with one another and make an effort to strive for peace in the relationship.

Scriptural Guidance on Relationships:

Child to Parent

Our first earthly relationship is with our parents. This is our foundation for understanding love and relationships. I was blessed to have a loving family. It was blessed because God was at the center of it. I grew up in a family that feared and respected the Lord. Knowing God's Will for the family according to His Word helps establish a proper family relationship, which in turn brings peace and harmony.

Unfortunately, sometimes this is not always a positive relationship and can set us on the wrong path about love and relationships. We must remember that God first loved us, even if our earthly parents do not show us the same. God can help us heal from hurt relationships from the past. Reach out for support and healing if you struggle in this area. If we do not reconcile our relationship with our parents, it will impact all other relationships in our lives.

In Exodus 20:12, God tells us that the key to a long life is by honoring your father and your mother. This is so essential that it is also the 5th of the Ten Commandments. Respecting our parents when we are young and even as we are adults is critical. If we disrespect our parents, we disrespect God who assigned them to us. Now, if your relationship with your parents is strained it should be addressed, but it should not come at the expense of respect.

Proverbs 1:8-9 advises children to hear the instruction of their fathers and listen to the teaching of their mothers. It states these should be worn like garland and pendants, without shame. Even when we are no longer children, we should be consulting the wisdom of our parents. They are the head of the relationship for a reason. Again, this is true if the parents espouse Godly truth and principles.

Parent to Child

Being a parent, especially for the first time, can be very overwhelming. You may think you are alone, but that is not true. God gives instructions on how to do this job that he has called you to. First and foremost, Proverbs 22:6 tells us that if we start our children on the right path, a path that is aligned to God's Will that, when they are old, they will not depart from it. Setting the Word of God into the hearts of children is the most important role as a parent. Although many, if not all, children will stray at some point in life, they will return if they have God's Word instilled inside them. We will always worry for our children and their well-being. While we should always pray for them, we also need to trust God's faithfulness in His Word that they will return to Him.

Although we perceive parenting mostly from a maternal perspective, many of the scriptures devoted to this relationship mention the father. Fathers play a very important role in the family structure.

Various research shows that many of the issues in society today stem from either an absent father or father who is not living up to his role in the family unit.

Scripture instructs us to not speak in anger to our children (Ephesians 6:4; Colossians 3:21), to correctively discipline them (Proverbs 13:24 and 29:17) and to give them wisdom (Deuteronomy 11:19; Proverbs 29:15). Scripture informs us that children are a heritage, an honor and a reward (Psalm 127:3). We should always encourage and love them.

Most importantly we need to be role models. We need to not just tell our children what to do and what not to do, but we must live out a Godly life for them to witness and follow. Titus 2:7 says, "in all things showing yourself *to be* a pattern of good works; in doctrine *showing* integrity, reverence, incorruptibility."

If we were set on the right path by our parents, then we should continue to pass that legacy on to our children and hold tight to it. If we were not given a righteous start, lean-in to God for guidance and ask Him to break that cycle with you. Break away from any generational curse of bad parenting and start your children on the right path. We do not have to parent the way we were parented unless we choose to. Raising our children on Godly principles will bring harmony and peace to the home.

Husband and Wife

Scripture mentions many instances about the unity of marriage and being husband and wife. In order for peace to exist in this relationship, God should be at the center of it and love must prevail in all circumstances. Ephesians 5:28 (NIV) says, "In the same way husbands should love their wives as their own bodies. He who loves his wife loves himself." Again, in Ephesians 5:33 (NIV), it tells us, "However, each one of you also must love his wife as he loves himself, and the wife must respect her husband." Mutual love and respect will carry a couple through difficult times. In 1 Peter 4:8 (ESV), it is not specifically referencing relationships of husband and wife, but it is a good rule of thumb. It states, "Above all, keep loving one another earnestly, since love covers a multitude of sins."

Forgiveness is also essential in marriage. We have all done wrong things and we cannot hold others accountable to perfection when we cannot achieve that ourselves. We need to show grace to our partner, just as we should receive it in return. That does not mean we should tolerate abuses of any kind. You should not be in a relationship where you feel unsafe. Seek help from professionals if you are dealing with this. In general, communication can be a tool in solving many misunderstandings.

Rather than making assumptions about motives or feelings, being open and honest in discussion can avoid many hurts and disappointments. Pray for one another and pray together. Satan is trying to divide what God has put together. Don't let him win. Let love win!

Authority to Subordinate

If we believe in divine appointments, then we must recognize that whether we like a particular person or not, they are in the position that God has allowed them to be placed in (Romans 13:1). These people are there for His purpose. We are to address them with respect whether we agree with them or not. First and foremost, we should pray for those in positions of authority, that they seek council from Godly people and make decisions that align with the Will of God.

In 1 Timothy 2:1-4 (ESV), it tells us, "First of all, then, I urge that supplications, prayers, intercessions, and thanksgivings be made for all people, ² for kings and all who are in high positions, that we may lead a peaceful and quiet life, godly and dignified in every way. ³ This is good, and it is pleasing in the sight of God our Savior, ⁴ who desires all people to be saved and to come to the knowledge of the truth." According to this scripture, living a peaceful and quiet life comes when we are in prayer and thankfulness for the people God has put in our paths.

This can be very difficult at times when we do not like or agree with these people. How we respond is a choice and a test for us. We cannot change them, but we can change ourselves. God blesses those who do not "lose their cool" when faced with opposition.

Again, we should not accept abuse or mistreatment from those who are in authority, but we should never harm or disrespect them. We can communicate our concerns, seek justice rightfully and distance ourselves from them if possible. Ultimately, it is for God to judge them based on their deeds.

Friend to Friend

God loves us so much, not only did He send us the best friend of all, Jesus, He also has given us many traveling companions so that we are not on this journey alone. Ecclesiastes 4:9-10 informs us, "Two *are* better than one because they have a good reward for their labor. [10] For if they fall, one will lift up his companion. But woe to him *who is* alone when he falls, For *he has* no one to help him up." God knows life can be difficult and wants us to be supported along the way.

While we should love and respect all those we interact with, nothing is sweeter than our "inner circle" of friends. It is said when you are young you have lots of friends and when you are older you can count your friends on one hand. These are your "inner circle friends". These are the friends you can call on, no matter what the circumstances are, and they will be there for support. Proverbs 27:9 (TPT) tells us, "a sweet friendship refreshes the soul." True friends are a blessing from God. Our inner circle should consist of people with Godly character and who speak life into our lives. (1 Corinthians 15:33) (Proverbs 16:28)

As it is with anything of value in life, friendships require attention, dedication and love. We should be praying for our friends according to their needs and investing in their lives. Proverbs 17:17 states, "a friend loves at all times, and a brother is born for a time of adversity." Often the encouragement from a close friend is what keeps us going in hard times. Sometimes the bonds of friendship grow stronger than those of family. We should honor our close friendships and thank God for them daily.

Our Enemy

Scripture even guides us on our relationships with our enemies. Jesus spoke very clearly about how to address this. In Matthew 5:43-47, Jesus said, "You have heard that it was said, 'Love your neighbor and hate your enemy.' [44] But I tell you, love your enemies and pray for those who persecute you, [45] that you may be children of your Father in heaven. He causes his sun to rise on the evil and the good, and sends rain on the righteous and the unrighteous. [46] If you love those who love you, what reward will you get? Are not even the tax collectors doing that? [47] And if you greet only your own people, what are you doing more than others? Do not even pagans do that?" Here Jesus is calling us to be set apart from non-believers by applying the Holy Spirit to love and pray for those who have hurt us. He wants us to extend beyond ourselves and be like Him, loving all people regardless of their actions.

Our job is not to seek revenge when we feel we have been wronged. In the end, that only harms us. God says the better way is to pray for those who have persecuted us and let Him handle it. We should consider paying back evil with good. Therefore, shining the Light of Christ. This is only possible if we gain God's perspective. When He looks at us, He doesn't see our sin, He sees His beautiful creation. In the same way, we should see God's creation in others and not their wrong-doings. This will help us to forgive and pray for the wrong they have done.

Relationships are like an intricate web. One strand moves and it impacts all the others. It is impossible to act completely independently without affecting the people around us, which is why this topic needs far more investigation that what is mentioned in this chapter. However, starting with God's Word for relationships gives us a foundation for how to interact appropriately in order to have balance and peace.

Hebrews 12:14 (NIV) states, "Make every effort to live in peace with everyone and to be holy; without holiness no one will see the Lord."

At the heart of any good relationship is communication. Recall all of the insights from the previous chapter and apply them to troubled relationships in your life.

      Lastly, it is very important that in all of our relationships, we are never the reason that someone stumbles. Paul warns us in Romans 14:13 (NIV), "Therefore let us stop passing judgment on one another. Instead, make up your mind not to put any stumbling block or obstacle in the way of a brother or sister." We must never intentionally be the reason someone fails. Revenge, sabotage, slander and lies can bring others down. God wants us to encourage one another and build each other up, not tear one another down. Not only will this bring peace to us, but it passes peace to others.

Reflection:

Who is in your inner circle?

Is there an unhealthy relationship in your life? If yes, how does God want you to handle this?

Who in your life needs to hear that you love and respect them?

Action Steps:

- Reach out to someone by phone or letter. Maybe it is a person whom you have not spoken to in a while. Let them know you are thinking of them and tell them how they have positively influenced your life.
- Mend a relationship that may have been wrongfully severed.

Finding Peace of Mind

"The mind governed by the flesh is death, but the mind governed by the Spirit is life and peace."

Romans 8:6, NIV

Key Insight: The devil has no power unless we give it to him.

Affirmation: My mind is my own and I choose to focus my mind on righteousness.

Think of your most precious possession. Would you just willingly hand it over to a thief? I am sure your answer would be *no*, you would resist it at all costs. Well, Satan is after our mind and we may be willingly giving it to him on a daily basis. We must ask ourselves two questions: How do we recognize this take-over? And how do we resist it? A friend of mine's son is a lawyer. She has told me countless times that he operates by the phrase, "If it ain't on the page, it ain't on the stage." In legal terms, if you don't have it in writing, it never happened. We must keep this is mind in all of our thoughts, words and actions. If God's Word doesn't support it, then we best not do it! Similarly, if scripture says it, then we should abide by it. God's Word should be the basis for all decisions.

God is not a god of confusion. He is a god of clarity. If we do not feel peace about an issue, then we know it is not from God. We must be able to recognize Satan's voice, but through the leading of the Holy Spirit we should be listening for God's voice and following it. This is the only way we can strive to be governed by The Spirit and not the flesh.

> *If it costs you your peace of mind, then the price is too high.*
> *-Unknown*

Like many women, I like pretty things. I give attention to how I dress and how I decorate my home. I thought this was making me happy. Don't get me wrong, there is nothing wrong with owning nice things. What I did not realize at first was that my motivation for having these nice things was totally out of alignment with God's Will for me. When I saw something I wanted, my mind would tell me it was okay to own it because I worked hard and I deserved it. So, I would give-in and treat myself to whatever was capturing my attention in the moment. Soon, shopping became my therapy and escape from the busy and often chaotic life that I was living at the time.

While this did not necessarily cause me to go into debt, it did put a stress on my finances, which in turn stole my peace in life. As I became stronger in my faith through the leading of the Holy Spirit, I realized that I had the wrong mode of thinking in this particular area and had to make a change. God did not want me to continue down this path of destructive behavior, He wanted me to correct my thinking. When I recognized that this was going against God's Will, it became clear to me that this was a sin. God directed me to James 4:17 (NIV), "If anyone, then, knows the good they ought to do and doesn't do it, it is sin for them."

The first thing I needed to do was gain control of my mind and the thoughts that dwelled in it. I had to admit and realize my wrongful thinking. Then, I needed to lean into God to reveal to me how to change. Remember, God wants us to choose Him, not be obligated to follow Him. Therefore, devotion to God has more power than duty to Him.

In order to change my behavior, I had to love God more than I wanted to embrace the wrong behavior. I knew I deeply loved God and He loved me, so I wanted to honor and obey him by setting my mind straight in this area. Once I made this choice, my spirit was strengthened and my mind followed. I was able to turn away from the destructive behavior almost immediately.

Obviously, I needed to follow-through with action, so I disengaged with all the places of temptation that would lead me to continue to sin in this area. I took a break from social media and unsubscribed to all the shopping sites where I became a frequent shopper.

Now if I buy something, it actually brings me joy instead of stress because I thought about the purchase and bought it with intention.

My testimony is similar to any type of addictive behavior. We think we want more of something, although that underlying desire is not for the right reasons and it could potentially harm us. So, how does our mind get set on the wrong path of thinking in the first place? If Satan can entice us through our flesh, then he begins to win over our mind. God gave us our senses so we can delight in His creation. Satan can hijack our senses to lead us down the wrong path. All along in my journey, Satan had been whispering lies to me, saying that I deserved the things I was buying and should indulge in frivolous spending. He convinced me it was okay after all because that's what everyone else was doing, right?

Romans 12:2 reminds us, "And do not be conformed to this world, but be transformed by the renewing of your mind, that you may prove what *is* that good and acceptable and perfect will of God." We are bombarded by images daily that do not represent Godly things. Slowly, these images start to corrode our perceptions and ultimately our mind. We need to have a filter for our own minds. Embracing the Holy Spirit that God has placed in us gives us power to overcome the mind and the flesh.

One slippery slope for the control of our mind comes from technology. Before I go on, I want to be clear that my intention is not to demonize technology. It has had tremendous benefits on our lives. However, since its creation, it has taken on a mind of its own and has been successful in leading people down paths they may not have otherwise found.

I remember learning the term **GIGO** back in middle school. This was the time when computers were really beginning to take off. In the technology field this stands for *Garbage In, Garbage Out*. Since computers can only do what they are told (well at that point in time anyway) they will act according to what is programmed into them. Our minds are very similar in this respect. If we are always filling it with junk, then we cannot expect fruitful outcomes. We need to be extremely cautious about what we allow into our minds. This includes what we watch, listen to and interact with daily.

One such example is the increased states of virtual reality, as seen through media, video games and other platforms. Virtual reality, in fact, has become an altered or alternative state of reality, not a simulation of actual reality. For illustrative purposes, let's imagine reality as levels. We live in the neutral position, or middle level. God is in the level above us and virtual reality is the level below us. When we dabble in the world of virtual reality, we put a bigger distance or gap between us and God. Flirting with this realm allows us to believe things that are not true. Eventually the lines between these levels become blurred and we can lose sight of what is unreal and what is real.

On a screen in an alternate realm, we can be someone else, have relations with strangers, kill people, steal things and the list goes on. My belief is that over time these lines fade and people's minds have a difficulty adjusting back to present reality, let alone God's reality. This creates dangerous thinking patterns and behaviors.

I want to emphasize that this is not a consequence necessarily of a one-time occurrence of something. It is when we develop a negative pattern of behavior that we start to distance ourselves from God. We think we are entertaining ourselves with these distractions, but we are really entertaining Satan, giving-in to sin, and losing our focus on God. This gives Satan power to do even more evil within us and the world.

However, the good news of Jesus' sacrifice takes care of Satan. In the end, he will not be victorious. Our job is to hold back while we remain on earth, not allowing him to operate within our life. Colossians 2:13-15 (NIV) tells us, "When you were dead in your sins and in the uncircumcision of your flesh, God made you alive with Christ. He forgave us all our sins, [14] having canceled the charge of our legal indebtedness, which stood against us and condemned us; he has taken it away, nailing it to the cross. [15] And having disarmed the powers and authorities, he made a public spectacle of them, triumphing over them by the cross." Through Jesus' death, our sins have been wiped away and God stripped power away from Satan.

So how is it that Satan is still able to act today? We need to constantly remind ourselves that this is a fallen world and we are living in Satan's territory. We are expecting things to be done right, but the world is operating under Satan's principles. The world is calling us to belong to it, but if we have said *"yes"* to Jesus, then we belong to God. The choice is ours to be part of the world or to be part of God's Kingdom here on earth. This requires us to think and act within God's principles. This will set-us apart from unbelievers.

We are told in John 17:14-16, "I have given them Your word; and the world has hated them because they are not of the world, just as I am not of the world. [15] I do not pray that You should take them out of the world, but that You should keep them from the evil one. [16] They are not of the world, just as I am not of the world." While we cannot change the world, we can change ourselves. We have to want to be set-apart from worldly thinking.

We fuel Satan's evil ways when we hand our minds over to things that do not align with God's Will. God gives us free will. He respects our ability to make choices. However, he makes it very clear that every choice has consequences and we are not immune to the impact of these consequences. If we choose to walk in God's Will then we are fruitful and goodness multiplies in our life and on the earth. When we walk in disobedience, darkness multiplies and we see a world that is out of alignment with God's Will. We have choice to move in the light or in darkness. If we want to experience peace, we must move in the light. Paul tells us in Philippians 2:13-16 (NIV), "for it is God who works in you to will and to act in order to fulfill His good purpose. [14] Do everything without grumbling or arguing, [15] so that you may become blameless and pure, "children of God without fault in a warped and crooked generation." Then you will shine among them like stars in the sky [16] as you hold firmly to the word of life. And then I will be able to boast on the day of Christ that I did not run or labor in vain."

I know that this book is meant to be uplifting and inspiring, however I want to be completely open here. There is a caveat to accepting this type of thinking. Once you truly commit to Jesus in all your ways, life on earth can become difficult because the world is not operating under the same principles as we are. People may distance themselves from you, accuse you of all sorts of things and you may experience persecution. We are told in 2 Timothy 3:12, "Yes, and all who desire to live godly in Christ Jesus will suffer persecution." Jesus himself was persecuted, so we should expect to be also.

We are called to be set apart and we may even be hated for His name's sake. John 15:19 states, "If you were of the world, the world would love its own. Yet because you are not of the world, but I chose you out of the world, therefore the world hates you." This does not mean we should be fearful or shrink back in being Christ-minded. I find the words of 1 Peter 5:10 extremely comforting,

"But may the God of all grace, who called us to His eternal glory by Christ Jesus, after you have suffered a while, perfect, establish, strengthen, and settle you." This is how we have peace; resting in God's grace and strength no matter what the circumstances are around us.

We must guard or hearts and minds daily by seeking God and His Word. This will encourage us and we should also encourage one another. Trusting the guidance of God through daily decision making will never lead us in the wrong direction. Proverbs 3:5 tells us, "Trust in the Lord with all your heart, and lean not on your own understanding." We do not have to "get it right", we need God to show us what is right. Knowing that we can trust God at all times brings about a wonderful sense of peace because we do not need to make decisions on our own. Peace doesn't mean there isn't chaos around us. Peace comes from our thoughts and reactions to those things. Choose to give God your mind and you will never go wrong. "You will keep in perfect peace those whose minds are steadfast, because they trust in you." (Isaiah 26:3, NIV)

Reflection:

Who has control of your thoughts?

Who/What are your sources of information for decision making?

Action Steps:

- Take an inventory of what occupies your mind.
- Disengage from potentially dangerous distractions.
- Stay connected with like-minded individuals and encourage each other.

Finding Peace Within Our Body

"Do you not know that your bodies are temples of the Holy Spirit, who is in you, whom you have received from God? You are not your own;"

1 Corinthians 6:19, NIV

Key Insight: Peace works from the inside out.

Affirmation: My body was designed by God and it should function according to His Will.

One of the most difficult things in life is to find peace when you have a chronic illness. I was diagnosed with a rare disorder several years ago. Actually, they call it the trifecta because it is three separate conditions that tend to manifest together. I suffered for eight years before finding the right doctor who could give me a proper diagnosis. Those years were filled with anxiety, pain, confusion and chaos. I spent countless hours doing research so I could treat myself. Not only did I lack peace, but it was robbing peace from everyone who was around me on a regular basis. I will not give too many details here because this is not a biography, but it is important to mention these things for the purpose of this testimony.

One day while I was on my way to teach a class, I started to feel strange. My eyes became blurry, my lips swelled and I had a rash all over my body. Next thing I knew, my throat was constricting and I was about to pass out. I was having an anaphylactic reaction, the severest form of an allergy, which could lead to death. I did not know this at the time because it had never happened to me before. All I knew was something wasn't right. I was on campus and I did not even know where the nurse's office was, but I knew I needed to find it quickly. I was divinely led straight to the building in front of me. I never had reason to enter this building before, but sure enough it was the building that housed the nurse's office. They got my situation under control and called for assistance. When the situation was under control, because of its severity, it was recommended that I visit a specialist.

That incident began my wild health adventure. After much testing, they could not determine what caused the reaction. I was warned to live a cautious life being aware of everything I would come in contact with. I was also trained on how to give myself life-saving medication, in case another reaction was to occur. Having been near death, your mind starts to play games with you. Fear sets-in quickly and panic often follows. I was diagnosed with PTSD, post-traumatic stress disorder because I would wake up in sweats and panic in the middle of the night thinking that I could not breath. While I had been working on my recovery, I lost over fifty pounds because I was scared to eat anything and risk another reaction.

My health was out of control and the stress of the entire situation nearly killed me.

About a year after the initial reaction, I was ill with an infection. Since I seemed to be allergic to everything, the doctors could not just follow the standard course of treatment. I needed to be under supervision at the hospital in order to be given medication to treat the infection. Sure enough, I began to have a reaction and they needed to stop the treatment. I was released from the hospital and was told to see another specialist the next day. When I got home that evening, I had a complete physical and mental breakdown. The doctors literally did not know what to do for me. When your life depends on someone and they cannot help you, where do you turn? If the infection was not treated, it would cause other major complications and who-knows-what would happen from there. I needed a miracle.

I remember sitting on my sofa crying out to Jesus for healing. I felt alone, helpless and so scared. In between my sobbing I noticed a warm sensation radiate through my body. It was as if electricity had passed through me. Once the feeling subsided, I had a great sense of peace. When I went to the specialist the next morning, they ran tests and discovered that the infection was gone. I did not need to take any medication or go for further treatment. Jesus had healed me.

While I am still dealing with mild issues from my original disorder, I have not taken any medication, not even an aspirin, nor have I needed it in almost ten years.

God began work in my body that night and He has made me better each day since. Once I knew that my healing was in God's hands and not the doctors', my faith increased and my sense of anxiety decreased.

God had set me on a path of healing that was providing me with peace of mind and peace within my body. I thank and praise God daily for his great works in me. In order to stay physically healthy, I needed to be sure to stay connected to God as my source for strength and healing. This began to happen as I prayed more earnestly, read God's Word more deeply, and handed over my worry about my health to Him.

My body was reacting to the way I was handling things on the inside, particularly stress. It is written in 3 John 1:2, "Beloved, I pray that you may prosper in all things and be in health, just as your soul prospers." Once my spirit was aligned with God, it did not matter what the condition of my body was; I still had peace.

Jesus tells us in John 14:27 that he has given us peace. That verse says, "Peace I leave with you, My peace I give to you; not as the world gives do I give to you. Let not your heart be troubled, neither let it be afraid." The key to peace is to not be troubled or afraid on the inside. There is nothing that can happen to us that Jesus cannot take care of. While God is working on the inside, we should still be caring for ourselves on the outside.

> *In a healthy body is a healthy spirit.*
>
> *— Czech Proverb*

From the outset, I want to emphasize that this chapter is not meant to dispense medical advice. It is for the purpose of awareness. It is said that prevention is the best medicine. Preventing our bodies from being in situations that cause us harm is the best way to stay healthy. God designed our bodies and knows what is best for it. Taking biblical guidance on health decisions is a wise choice. With that being said, it is important to consult with sound medical advice for information and ultimately make a decision that gives you peace.

Biblical insights about our bodies is not meant to be restrictive or a means to deny us of things. It is for our protection. Proverbs 4:20-22 tells us, "My son, give attention to my words; Incline your ear to my sayings. [21] Do not let them depart from your eyes; Keep them in the midst of your heart; [22] For they *are* life to those who find them, And health to all their flesh." Just as we take daily vitamins to strengthen our physical body, taking in The Word of God daily strengthens our spirit, heart and mind. If our spirit, heart and mind are in the right place, then our body will follow.

Proverbs 3:7-8 states, "Do not be wise in your own eyes; Fear the LORD and depart from evil. [8] It will be health to your flesh, And strength to your bones." God's Word gives specific instructions for how our bodies can be in alignment with His Will. There is practically a verse for every part of our body. When we follow God's advice for how to treat our bodies, our health will begin to fall in place. For ease of reference, I will bullet point some of the scriptures below relating to health and the body.

Guard your eyes- Be cautious of what you watch and view.

- Matthew 6:22, "The lamp of the body is the eye. If therefore your eye is good, your whole body will be full of light."

Guard your ears- Be cautious of who and what we listen to.

- Proverbs 23:12, "Apply your heart to instruction, And your ears to words of knowledge."

Guard your heart- Keep it pure and clean.

- Proverbs 4:23, "Keep your heart with all diligence, For out of it *spring* the issues of life."

Sexual Immorality- this destroys the temple of God.*

- 1 Corinthians 6:18 (NIV), "Flee from sexual immorality. All other sins a person commits are outside the body, but whoever sins sexually, sins against their own body."

*It is interesting to note that in many cases in scripture, when sins are mentioned, often sexual immorality is listed first. We know all sins are equal, yet sexual immorality is the defilement of the temple of the Holy Spirit and this is quite significant.

Food and Drink- earthly food and drink only satisfies the flesh; let it not become a focus of our being.

- 1 Corinthians 10:31 (NIV), "So whether you eat or drink or whatever you do, do it all for the glory of God."
- Matthew 4:4, "But He (Jesus) answered and said, "It is written, 'Man shall not live by bread alone, but by every word that proceeds from the mouth of God"

Exercise/Physical Appearance- God is more concerned about what is inside than how you look on the outside.

- 1 Timothy 4:8 (ESV), "For while bodily training is of some value, godliness is of value in every way, as it holds promise for the present life and also for the life to come."

- 1 Samuel 16:7, "But the LORD said to Samuel, "Do not look at his appearance or at his physical stature, because I have refused him. For *the LORD does* not *see* as man sees; for man looks at the outward appearance, but the LORD looks at the heart."

Rest- Rest is not just physically important, it also renews our soul. Even God rested.

- Hebrews 4:9-11, "There remains therefore a rest for the people of God. [10] For he who has entered His rest has himself also ceased from his works as God *did* from His."
- Matthew 11:28-30, "Come to Me, all *you* who labor and are heavy laden, and I will give you rest. [29] Take My yoke upon you and learn from Me, for I am gentle and lowly in heart, and you will find rest for your souls. [30] For My yoke *is* easy and My burden is light."

Paul implores us in Romans 12:1, "I beseech you therefore, brethren, by the mercies of God, that you present your bodies a living sacrifice, holy, acceptable to God, *which is* your reasonable service." Giving ourselves over to God's Will allows Him to work through us. He will prepare our hearts, minds and bodies for the good works He has for us. If we are unwell, we may not be as effective as we could be for His purpose. Jesus tells us in Matthew

13:15, "For the hearts of this people have grown dull. *Their* ears are hard of hearing, And their eyes they have closed, Lest they should see with *their* eyes and hear with *their* ears, Lest they should understand with *their* hearts and turn, so that I should heal them." We need to turn toward Jesus in order for Him to heal us in all ways.

      Jesus endured wounds so that we may be healed (Isaiah 53:5). This was for restoration of our soul and our body. We must not forget that Jesus understands what we are going through since he took human form and walked the earth. He knew we would need a helper, so God sent us the Holy Spirit (John 14:16 & 26). Acknowledging that The Holy Spirit dwells inside of us can give us strength to endure the physical limitations and illness we might experience here on earth. Remember daily that Jesus suffered so we can be saved from sin that destroys our body and our spirit. We can live in peace knowing that Jesus works from the inside-out.

Reflection:

How are you caring for the temple of your spirit?

What areas require more attention?

Action Steps:

- Pray specifically to God for the healing that you require. Believe He is healing you and receive it.
- Focus on the peace of Jesus.
- Visualize your body being whole, healed and well.
- Be sure to give your body rest.

Finding Peace Within Our Spirit

"And I will ask the Father, and he will give you another advocate to help you and be with you forever…"

John 14:16, NIV

Key Insight: You are not in this alone. God has sent you a helper, the Holy Spirit.

Affirmation: My spirit is fueled by the power of the Holy Spirit.

    It was a warm and sunny Monday in early fall. I was about to have my first child and I was on my way to the hospital. So many feelings ran through my mind at this time, it was difficult to focus on any one particular thing. Questions raced so quickly that I could barely hold on to one before the next one filled my mind. Will I be in pain? Will the baby be okay? Will I be a good mom? After hours on a roller coaster ride of extremes, a beautiful new life entered into the world. It was 5:25 on Monday, September 10, 2001. My husband and I celebrated what would be the most joyous day of our lives.

We went to sleep peacefully that night because our baby was here. He was safe and healthy, and tomorrow would be the beginning of our new life together.

Will there be another attack? That was not one of the questions that raced through my mind the previous day because that was September 10th, and terrorism was not a daily word yet. However, this was September 11th and the world had changed overnight. When my husband came to join me again at the hospital that morning we were glued to the television as the events of the day were just unfolding. We felt the joy of yesterday begin to slip away and the fear of today start to take residence.

We were in a Jewish hospital in New York City. We were told that we were a target for potential attack and the hospital was on complete lock down. They needed to prepare for the potential victims that would be arriving after the attacks. There was no phone service and we could not get in touch with the outside world. Now different questions raced through my mind: Will we be safe? Where will we go? What kind of world did I bring this child into?

The television screen above our son's bassinette glowed with horrific images of death, despair and destruction, while lying below it was our beautiful newborn son full of hope and life. The doctor came to exam him. All the while, he was concerned for his own family who worked in the proximity of the towers. At that moment, we told the doctor to please go check on his family, as our son was just fine.

How many families were broken apart and forever changed that day? It was then and there that we had to make a decision. Would we give into the despair that could have easily overtaken us, or would we press into the hope that God just bestowed upon us through our new son? We prayed like never before for God's protection, provision, and most of all, His guidance as we navigated this completely unexpected path that we found ourselves on.

There is plenty to learn in parenting and it is difficult enough being a new parent when you know the parameters in which you are operating. However, from our perspective, the future was unsure and quite scary. We simply could not rely on our own perspective or understanding if we wanted to successfully move forward. We had to commit to seeking God's perspective as stated in Proverbs 3:5-6 (NIV), "Trust in the LORD with all your heart and lean not on your own understanding; [6] in all your ways submit to him, and he will make your paths straight."

Many lessons revealed themselves over the next few months and years. Not just practical parenting lessons, but lessons on the dependence of God. Adversity often provides opportunities for spiritual growth. This was one of those such times. The overwhelming uncertainty of all the events we were observing around us led us to seek something beyond that.

First and foremost, we learned to focus on our Savior and not our situation. This mindset shift brings automatic peace to any circumstance. We cannot control the events that happen, but we can stay close to the one who has control. Connecting on an intimate level with the Holy Spirit brings a wave of peace like nothing else can. God sent The Holy Spirit to dwell in us so we can have a direct connection to Him at all times. Daily opportunities to quiet the chaos and connect with God boosts our ability to handle whatever is in front of us.

As mentioned in a previous chapter, we must understand that this is a fallen world and that Satan has dominion over it, but God has not left us nor forsaken us (Deuteronomy 31:6). His Holy Spirit is with us so we can discern situations, make righteous decisions and have comfort during our trials. Knowing that Satan has dominion on the earth makes us aware of the fact that opposites will exist. So, if there is good then there must be bad. If there is up, then there is down. If there is success, then there is failure. My earthly father would always say, "Things are never as good or as bad as they seem." I believe that peace lives between these extremes.

Acknowledging and accepting this fact helps us to deal with disappointment better so our spirit does not get crushed. Life is not always going to be consistently one way or the other. It will flow back and forth in order to keep a balance. To not get tossed about in life's ups and downs, we need to stay anchored to God through the Holy Spirit. This alone should begin to give us daily comfort and peace.

I want to address a common fallacy here. I am sure you have heard the saying, "God doesn't give you more than you can handle." Well, this is not entirely true. People who say this are leaving off the most important part of this statement. It should be, "God doesn't give you more than you can handle, with His help." Apart from full reliance on God, we truly cannot do anything. As our relationship and reliance on God grows, our spirit will begin to transform us from being a *What-if* person to an *Even-if* person.

The *What-if* person may be anxious, fearful or unsettled by life's events. Always wondering *What-if* something goes wrong causes stress and unrest in our lives. This type of person tries to retain control and take matters into their own hands often to no avail. Challenges in life tend to be bigger than we can handle, but our God is bigger than our challenges.

Being an *Even-if* person turns control over to God and rests in the fact that no matter what the situation looks like, He has our back. *Even if* things look uncertain or impossible, God is in control. Lifting that burden off ourselves provides tremendous peace.

Ego says, "Once everything falls into place, I'll feel peace." Spirit says, "Find your peace and then everything will fall into place."
— Marianne Williamson

Just as we feed our bodies for optimum results, we need a spiritual diet as well. I already discussed the need for the daily plug-in and connection with the Holy Spirit. Reading God's Word daily strengthens our spirits so we can handle the challenges of the day. We need to recharge our spirit and realize the power it has. In 1 John 4:4 (NIV), we are told, "You, dear children, are from God and have overcome them, because the one who is in you is greater than the one who is in the world." Within us is a spirit that can overcome the challenges of the world.

In addition, we should strive to put on the Full Armor of God each day as described in Ephesians 6:10-18. This will give us the courage and tools we need to stand, no matter what life throws at us. Being protected by the Armor of God sends a message to Satan that the Holy Spirit dwells in us and there is no vacancy for him to take residence in.

However, do not be mistaken, this is a daily battle. Satan will look for any crack or crevice to enter your life and wreak havoc. We must make sure every earthly and spiritual door is closed to him. The Holy Spirit will convict and minister to us in the areas of our life where we need to make changes. Sometimes, we might recognize this as a "gut" instinct, but it is really the nudge of the Holy Spirit warning us about which way to go.

Going back to my testimony earlier in this chapter, as I write this book, my son is 18 years old, he is a successful college student who is respectful, intelligent and creative.

Most importantly he loves the Lord and is fully aware of how his parents weathered a very difficult time in American history. We were never alone. The grace and peace of God had led us at each turn and continues to do so. Be encouraged because God is with you, and if He is for you, who then can be against you? (Romans 8:31)

Reflection:

When was a time that you really needed to press-in to God for the power of the Holy Spirit to work in your life? How did God respond?

Is there something you are currently dealing with that you need to overcome?

Action Steps:

- Turn your **What-if** statements into **Even-if** statements.
- Fix your eyes on **the Savior** and not the situation.
- Let Go and **Let God** work in your situation.
- Put on the Full Armor of God each day. (To learn more about the Armor of God, see the chart in the Appendix.)
- Let the Holy Spirit nudge you in the right direction.

Finding Peace for Provision

"The thief does not come except to steal, and to kill, and to destroy. I have come that they may have life, and that they may have it more abundantly."

John 10:10

Key Insight: Jesus is enough. Seek contentment and demonstrate gratitude.

Affirmation: I have all that I need through God's supernatural provision.

The thief mentioned in John 10:10 is Satan. His only goal is to take the blessings from you that God has planned for you. This refers to both your natural and spiritual blessings. However, Jesus tells us in this same verse that He has come so we can have fullness of life and abundance. This abundance is not only for earthly things, but spiritual things as well. God wants us to have an abundant life both in this life and beyond. So, how do we tap into this abundance? We must trust Him at all times.

We cannot hold onto fear or worry and also have trust and peace. These things are in opposition of one another. If we are constantly worried about how to make ends meet, then we are not fully trusting God to provide. If we are worried about getting that new job that we interviewed for, then we are not fully trusting God. If we are fearful about the future, then we are not fully trusting God. This fear and worry chips away at our peace but trusting in God will bring us just the right thing at exactly the right time. With that being said, it is important to remember that building trust in God is a process that takes time to develop. God makes many promises in scripture and He can be trusted to honor every one of them.

I want to emphasize that God does not promise us that we will have all that we want, but he does tell us he will provide all that we need. In Philippians 4:19, Paul tells us, "And my God shall supply all your need according to His riches in glory by Christ Jesus." Jesus should always be our primary role model for our lives and He exhibited belief in this promise of God to its fullest extent. The Apostle Paul was also an excellent example in this regard. He learned how to earnestly depend on God's provision, no matter the circumstance.

Where God guides, God provides.

Paul's journeys were filled with numerous obstacles as he traveled continually to spread the Gospel over many lands. He never once worried about where his provision would come from. There was always someone along his route to house him, feed him, or support his ministry. He was within the Will of God and God provided for Paul. In 2 Corinthians 9:8, he tells us, "And God *is* able to make all grace abound toward you, that you, always having all sufficiency in all *things,* may have an abundance for every good work." God will give us everything we need to fulfill our purpose in Him. Being in God's Will and trusting Him is key.

Paul speaks about this beautifully in Philippians 4:11-13 (NIV), as he shares the secret to his ability to fully rely on God. He states, "I am not saying this because I am in need, for I have learned to be content whatever the circumstances. [12] I know what it is to be in need, and I know what it is to have plenty. I have learned the secret of being content in any and every situation, whether well fed or hungry, whether living in plenty or in want. [13] I can do all this through Him who gives me strength." Paul trusted and relied on God completely. He knew his strength was in his faith in Christ. No matter what Paul encountered, Jesus was enough for him.

Therefore, contentment in Jesus is the key to seeing God's Hand for provision in your life. Let us continually be thankful for all the big and little blessings in our lives. I say to be thankful for everything from "breath to bread." We need to show gratitude to God from the moment our eyes open in the morning to the moment they close at night. Being content and knowing Jesus is enough brings peace.

I can provide countless testimonies about this promise of God. Ever since I was young, I can remember seeing the Hand of God make provision. Actually, now as an adult, I can say this is practically a daily occurrence. One of the most impressionable instances happened when I was around 10 years old. My earthly father was the main "bread winner" for my family. He did rather well in this respect and I never needed or wanted for anything. Suddenly he lost his job and we hit a rough spot. We thought it would be temporary, but it lasted longer than we anticipated. There were times when we were literally wondering how to pay for dinner. Yet, by the end of each day, there was always a provision, whether it was someone preparing a meal, giving us grocery items or even unexpected financial gifts.

My parents were sure to emphasize in these instances that the grace of God made these provisions. This was not merely an obligatory confession of thanks, but an earnest belief that the Hand of God supernaturally provided for our earthly needs. Even at the age of 10, I was keenly aware that for something to occur once, it could be considered a coincidence; but a continual experience of unsolicited events requires a better explanation.

As of result of these experiences, I grew to always be thankful and to be expectant. I saw God work in our life and I knew he would do it again. Therefore, I learned to trust Him continually, no matter what the earthly circumstances looked like. This developed a spirit of gratitude and helped keep things in perspective, which then allows for you to experience peace. Never taking anything for granted is a fundamental turning point in this transformation of perspective. We have to realize that apart from God, we are nothing.

One practical way we can work on our perspective is by changing our thoughts, and ultimately, our words. As mentioned in a previous chapter, words have power. We can have more peace in our day by taking on a new perspective and moving from an "*I have to...*" to an "*I get to...*" mindset.

Let me elaborate on this. I can look at a pile of dishes in the sink and say, "Oh, *I have to* clean all these dishes" or I can say, "Oh, *I get to* clean these dishes and I am so glad my family and I had food to eat today." Similarly, I can think to myself, "Oh man, *I have to go* to work tomorrow", or I can think, "Oh man, *I get to* go to work tomorrow, which helps me to support my family." It is all about perspective. Building a perspective of continual gratitude helps us have peace over our provision.

While it is impossible to fully fathom God's perspective in our limited scope of human understanding, if we stay close to His Word, we start to see things the way he sees things and that changes our perspective here on earth. One of the ways that we can get closer to His perspective is through prayer. Philippians 4:6-7 (NIV) reminds us, "Do not be anxious about anything, but in every situation, by prayer and petition, with thanksgiving, present your requests to God. And the peace of God, which transcends all understanding, will guard your hearts and your minds in Christ Jesus." Praying to God for provision recognizes that He is the source of the provision. Our prayers in this area should begin with thanks for all the blessings that He has already provided. Even on our worst day, there is still something to be thankful for.

I have learned to depend on **GPS** to get through each day: **G**od's **P**rovision and **S**trength. Pressing into God daily aligns us more and more to His grace and abundance. We are told in Matthew 6:33, "Seek first the Kingdom of God and His righteousness, and all these things shall be added to you." It is easy to fall into the trap of believing that we have and get what we have from our own efforts. While we absolutely have to work for what we need, it is God in His grace who gives us the ability to receive these blessings. We are told in Deuteronomy 8:18 that it is because of God that we are able to work. It states, "And you shall remember the LORD your God, for *it is* He who gives you power to get wealth, that He may establish His covenant which He swore to your fathers, as *it is* this day." Opportunities present themselves according to God's Will, which then allows for us to reap these benefits.

So, contentment and gratitude give us peace, but blessing others helps us keep our peace. We are not blessed in order to hoard what we have been given. Again, this is true for both natural and spiritual blessings. We are blessed so we can be a blessing to others. God expects us to give much if we have received much! (Luke 12:48).

Think back to the testimony I shared earlier in this chapter. If anyone would have held back their blessings, then my family would not have been blessed. We are living witnesses of God. We need to be able to pay forward all that He has given to us. When we give to others, it helps to remind us of how much we truly have. God is always faithful to replenish our supply if we do what is right with our blessings.

Reflection:

What need do you have that you are anxious about?

In which areas of your life do you need to trust God more?

How can you help bless someone else with provision?

Action Steps:

- Express gratitude daily for all the little and big blessings (Breath to Bread).
- Transform your perspective from **Have-to**, to **Get-To.** Make a list if you need a reminder.
- Be generous. Don't just count your blessings, share them!

Finding Peace Over Timing

"My times are in your hands; deliver me from the hands of my enemies, from those who pursue me."

Psalms 31:15, NIV

Key Point: We cannot control time, but we can certainly manage it.

Affirmation: I will trust in God's timing.

    God had a lot of work to do with me when it came to this area of my life. I was obsessed with controlling time. I was glued to my agenda. I wrote a list for everything and I was easily bent out of shape if my schedule changed unexpectedly. Time is another aspect of God's provision. He can give it and he can take it away. It is a foolish pursuit to believe that we or any human can control time. However, that does not mean we cannot manage it.

    Just like all the other blessings that God has provided us with, we should be good stewards of the time he has given us. We are reminded often in the Bible to use our time wisely. Psalms 90:12 states, "So teach us to number our days, that we may gain a heart of wisdom."

One day while I was cooking in my kitchen, my mind, as usual, was racing back and forth over the list in my head of all the things I still needed to accomplish that day. God spoke clearly to me and said, *"Put life before the list."* He revealed to me several places where I needed to make changes in how I was spending my time. The first step was to spend time with Him first and then move on to other things. The call from God was so clear that I was immediately obedient. I began to reorder my time and my priorities, starting with putting God first. What happened was amazing. God redeemed my time. Once I started on this new routine, I was more focused, more energized and got more accomplished each day. But most of all, I was not as stressed as I had been and that gave me peace.

God's time is not our time. Since God owns time, he can arrange it how he sees fit. Time can slow down or speed up depending on God's Will. What is a challenge for us is to gain more of God's perspective concerning time. Waiting on God can seem like eternity. Our focus needs to be on trusting Him, no matter how long something takes to happen. Peace comes in knowing that God will fulfill all that he has promised, whether it be tomorrow or on our last breath. God is never early or late—He is always on time!

We learn through the stories of many biblical figures that God does not necessarily work quickly from an earthly perspective. Joseph was held captive for 14 years. Abraham waited 25 years for his promise. Moses wandered 40 years in the wilderness. It took approximately 50 years for Noah to build the ark. Yet the ending of all their stories are marked with greatness. God's timeline can be very stressful for us. It can seem like nothing is happening while waiting on God, especially during difficult times. But do not be fooled; God is working and getting all the details in order while we wait. Patience in the waiting will produce peace.

We simply cannot artificially move time on our own. God's blessing must be behind it. From the outset, if we fix our mind on God's perspective of time, we can alleviate much of the stress we feel in the day-to-day. Total trust in God and his timing will produce a much more peaceful existence for all of us. What we do in the waiting time is what will influence the outcomes in our lives. Jesus told us in Matthew 6:34 (NIV), "Therefore do not worry about tomorrow, for tomorrow will worry about itself. Each day has enough trouble of its own." The key is to stay focused on God and not worry because He is working things out on our behalf. While waiting we can pray, read the Word and engage with other believers so that we stay grounded and focused.

In the previous chapter about Peace within our Spirit, I shared with you the testimony about my son being born the day before the September 11th attack. Surely, I would not have chosen that time for him to be born, but God did. Almost immediately after that unprecedented time in American history, my family and I decided that we should pursue leaving New York City. We collectively, with God's guidance, believed that this was the correct thing to do. We actively sought to move in that direction for nearly 18 years. There were moments when it seemed likely it would happen and then it would fall through. Whether due to personal events or the general climate of the moment, the right time never seemed to arise.

There were times during the waiting that we considered giving up on moving at all. We continued to pray and believe in the promise that God showed us about our relocation. We knew we needed to press into God because he had something better in store. Then, just like that, after nearly 18 years of working and waiting, God opened the door for us to relocate. It was a seamless and relatively stress-free transition. We literally experienced supernatural intervention that moved time, space and opportunity simultaneously in order to manifest God's promise. Our faithfulness in God's timing not only brought about God's blessing, but it provided us with peace in the process. If we had tried to relocate earlier without the favor of God, it could have been a disaster rather than a blessing.

Sometimes you will never know the value of a moment until it becomes a memory.
                                                    -Ted Geisel

---

Our time is in God's hands, and no matter how we think we influence time, it does not change this fact. We may not agree or understand, but we are exactly where we are supposed to be at any given moment. There are countless testimonies of people who were seemingly at the right place at the right time to experience a blessing or were swiftly moved from a situation that could have had a serious negative consequence. Some might say this is coincidence, but that is the Hand of God orchestrating time. Albert Einstein once said, "Coincidence is God's way of remaining anonymous." Nothing on this planet happens without God being aware of it.

Let's learn to live in the moment. If we are always looking for the next thing, then we are never really living in the moment where God has currently placed us. This mindset robs us of the joys and blessings of the present day. Ecclesiastes 3:11 (NIV) tells us, "He has made everything beautiful in its time. He has also set eternity in the human heart; yet no one can fathom what God has done from beginning to end." Truly everything has a time and God's timing is perfect. God's perspective can see much farther and wider than our own. Pretending to even comprehend a fraction of His perspective, as it relates to time, is a foolish endeavor.

One thing we can understand is that this physical life on earth is relatively short. In order to make that time peaceful, we need to learn to measure it by the beautiful moments He gives us and not by the minutes of a clock or days on a calendar.

Reflection:

Are there any distractions that are cheating you out of time?

Does your schedule align with God's purpose?

Is there a particular situation where you need to build more patience?

How can you be productive while you are waiting on the Lord?

Was there a time when patience and waiting on God paid-off?

Action Steps:

- Look over schedules and agendas for priorities, find a planner that fits your purpose.
  (I recommend The Prayerful Planner, https://www.prayerfulplanner.com/)
- Set goals that align with God's will and purpose for your life.
- Don't give up.

Finding Peace Through Forgiveness

"Bearing with one another, and forgiving one another, if anyone has a complaint against another; even as Christ forgave you, so you also must do."

Colossians 3:13

Key Insight: Thank you God that you do not deal with me according to my sin, but you handle me with grace, mercy and forgiveness.

Affirmation: I will release forgiveness to others because God has been merciful to me.

We have all sinned. Anytime we are not in alignment with God's Will, we have sinned. Our thoughts, words and deeds have fallen short and sin separates us from God. God understood this and that is why he sent Jesus, our Savior. While Jesus was on earth, he confronted all the issues we face today, yet he never sinned. Jesus was perfect because he never thought or acted outside of God's Will. The sacrifice of Christ's perfect and sinless life for our sin was an uneven exchange. Yet, Jesus loved us so much that He was willing to make this sacrifice.

Understanding the magnitude of the forgiveness that we received from this sacrifice is life altering. Christ's blood has cleansed us in God's sight allowing us to have a relationship with Him.

There are several implications for understanding and receiving this forgiveness. First and foremost, we are to praise and thank God for this gift to be set free from the bondage of sin. It is truly a gift because there is no way we could earn this on our own (Ephesians 2:8-9). God loves us and wants us to be saved. There is nothing we can do that can separate us from His love. This is the beauty of a relationship with God through Christ. It is not about being compliant to follow a list of rules and laws, but rather our reciprocal love for God makes us want to be righteous in His eyes. Once we accept God's gift, He empowers The Holy Spirit to work inside of us to lead us away from temptation and be steered away from sin.

Second, through our will and the power of the Holy Spirit, we must make every effort to sin no more. One of the most sobering verses in the Bible is Hebrews 10:26 (NIV), "If we deliberately keep on sinning after we have received the knowledge of the truth, no sacrifice for sins is left." God already laid everything on the line for us. He gave us His only son for our salvation and gave us The Holy Spirit to help us. We should not know something is sinful and willfully continue to do it; this is apostasy. Living a life in this manner will destroy our body, mind, soul and relationship with God. Surely there will not be peace following this kind of lifestyle.

Sins are like the weeds in a garden; they tend to grow faster than the plants. If weeds are not attended to regularly and held back, they will eventually choke out the plants that are producing fruit. Therefore, the plant will never meet its potential. If we are dealing with sin that has taken root, we need to confess it to God, ask for forgiveness and repent. Repentance means to turn away from that thought or behavior and do it no more. Psalms 34:14 advises us, "Depart from evil and do good; Seek peace and pursue it." Ultimately, sin chokes out the potential God has for our life. Let us strive to live a life that honors God. This will lead us to peace.

Lastly, knowing that we have been forgiven should give us a heart to forgive others. Jesus gives a wonderful example of this in John 8:1-7 when he saves the adulterous women. Jesus says in verse 7, "He who is without sin among you, let him throw a stone at her first." This is a reminder to us that we have all sinned and we need to show grace to others when they fall, just as God has shown to us. Often, we are so quick to judge others for the wrongs they do but fail to see the errors we have made (Matthew 7:3). Harboring unforgiveness towards others grows animosity and allows negative thoughts and behaviors to cling to us. We must shed these thoughts and behaviors through forgiveness. We need to learn to forgive past, present and future wrongs of others. Matthew 6:14-15 (NIV) reminds us, "For if you forgive other people when they sin against you, your heavenly Father will also forgive you. [15] But if you do not forgive others their sins, your Father will not forgive your sins."

One mistake we often make is a comparison of our sinful nature to others. We rank sins according to how bad we think they are and hold others who have committed these sins to a different set of standards than ourselves. One can say, "Well, I am not as bad as so and so because I did not..." We must understand that no individual sin is worse than any other. When we compare our sins to someone else's sins, we fall far below God's standard. God's Word, not ours, is the yardstick for measuring all truth and behavior.

Most people will identify with the laws that were given to us in the Ten Commandments. For many, this is the standard with which they base sinfulness. If we keep to these commandments then we are doing okay, right? Well, which of the ten have we broken or continually break? Jesus teaches us that sin begins in our heart. He speaks about the Ten Commandments and elaborates in Matthew 5:21-22 by saying, "You have heard that it was said to those of old, 'You shall not murder, and whoever murders will be in danger of the judgment.' [22] But I say to you that whoever is angry with his brother without a cause shall be in danger of the judgment." Jesus goes on to tell us in Matthew 5:27-28, "You have heard that it was said to those of old, 'You shall not commit adultery.' [28] But I say to you that whoever looks at a woman to lust for her has already committed adultery with her in his heart." Even before we act, our thoughts have committed sin. We must recognize this and have repentance in our heart to experience real peace from forgiveness.

We learn from scripture that even the disciples, Jesus' followers, who were the closest people to Him on earth, sinned against Him. Now, betraying the Son of God…that is a big sin, right? Yet, Jesus forgave them. While dying on the cross, Christ even forgave a thief who was crucified along-side Him. He was forgiven because he repented and recognized that Jesus was his savior. Thank God our story does not end with our sin. We are told, that through the mystery of grace through faith, we are saved. If you have not accepted Jesus into your life as your personal savior, I implore you to do so. Romans 10:9-10 tells us, "that if you confess with your mouth the Lord Jesus and believe in your heart that God has raised Him from the dead, you will be saved. [10] For with the heart one believes unto righteousness, and with the mouth confession is made unto salvation."

Therefore, because of our sinful nature, we need the forgiveness that only Jesus, our Savior, can provide. Because we are forgiven and not condemned, we should extend the same grace to others. Knowing we are forgiven brings us peace. Forgiving others helps us keep our peace.

Let us forgive each other-only then will we live in peace.
— Leo Tolstoy

Reflection:

Is there someone who you need to forgive?

Are you waiting on forgiveness from someone else?

Action Steps:

- If you haven't already done so, accept Jesus as your savior. (There are simple steps in the appendix)
- Repent and change any wrongful ways.
- Extend forgiveness to someone who you have been holding back from.
- Earnestly ask God to release the burden of this unforgiveness. Feel the weight lift from you.

Closing Thoughts

"Whatever you have learned or received or heard from me, or seen in me—put it into practice. And the God of peace will be with you."

Philippians 4:9, NIV

Paul speaks in Philippians 4:9 about the peace found from following the instruction Jesus gave us. It is not enough to just hear these instructions, we must apply them as well. While in this case, practice might not make us perfect, one thing is for sure; we are not in this alone and God will never abandon us if we choose Him. Leaning on His strength will allow us to handle the many challenging situations we encounter in our lives. God's Word provides us with every insight necessary to live a life of peace. It is for us to hold tight to the Word and tune-out the world.

If you look at the world, you'll be distressed. If you look within, you'll be depressed. But if you look at Christ, you'll be at rest.
                                        -Corrie Ten Boom

I cannot over emphasize that peace does not come from things on the outside being perfect. Peace comes from how we deal with those things on the inside. It is not mentioned in scripture, nor did I suggest anywhere in this text that this is easy. However, that does not mean it is impossible to achieve. God would not set something in front of us that we could not obtain, nor place a desire within us that He could not fill. Neither can He just hand it over without us working for it, or no value will have been gained.

Hebrews 12:11 states, "Now no chastening seems to be joyful for the present, but painful; nevertheless, afterward it yields the peaceable fruit of righteousness to those who have been trained by it." Refining ourselves daily and continually moving toward God's Will, rather than away from it, will yield a life of righteousness and peace.

Peace in life comes from what we sow. James 3:18 (NIV) reminds us, "Peacemakers who sow in peace reap a harvest of righteousness." This is a continual process of sowing in good things so that we can reap good things. Strive every day to be just a little closer to God's Will than the day before. Remember God's grace and extend it to yourself when you fall, and to others when they need it. The only time we fail is when we give up. Never give up seeking His face and His peace will be upon you.

Our peace comes from a place higher than ourselves or this world. Looking to God through the connection with the Holy Spirit is our only hope for a life of peace, joy and abundance. Through our choice of saying *yes* to God, we are choosing to find peace on purpose.

May God continue to bless you on your journey of discovering His peace.

Appendix

I. Instructions for Creating A Vision Board

- Start with images, quotes or verses that represent the things you would like to do and accomplish. You can either clip them from magazines or print from online.
- Arrange them in an order that speaks to you.
- Once you have an arrangement, find a sturdy type of paper, either poster board or cardstock. The size of the paper will depend on how many images you have.
- Adhere them on the paper/board in the manner you organized them.
- Hang the board in a visible place so you can refer to and be inspired by it daily.
- Check the board often to see if you are moving towards your goals.
- If you have new ideas to add you can add them to original or make a new board.
- Feel free to create more than one board if you would like to keep ideas or aspects of your life separate.

Below is a photo of one of my vision boards. I found that after six months of creating the board, when I looked back, it was like a checklist. It kept me on track and I was able to celebrate moving in the direction of my goals and my purpose.

II.   Armor of God Challenge

Use this chart below to help keep track of your daily battle plan while putting on the armor of God.

Source: https://www.prayerfulplanner.com/

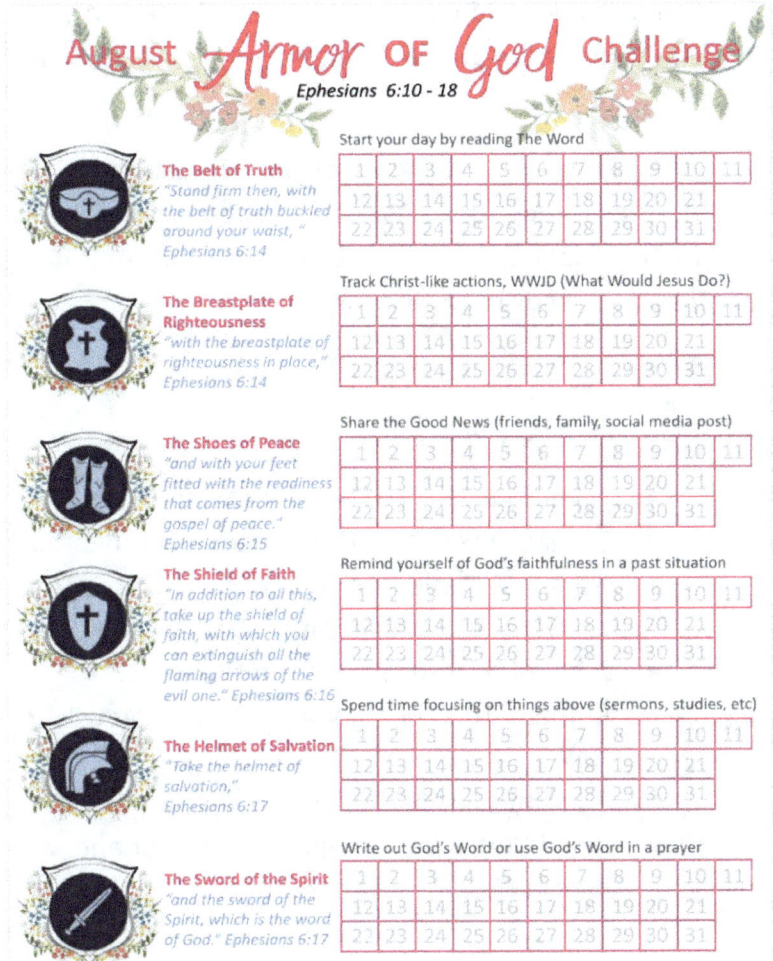

III.   Road to Salvation (Roman's Road)

If you are earnestly seeking forgiveness and a relationship with Jesus Christ, you can follow the steps below. It is called Roman's Road because the first steps are found in the book of Romans in the New Testament. The Apostle Paul speaks on how to be saved by faith through grace.

First, we need to admit we are sinners. We all need a savior, Jesus died for us. We must repent of our old ways and be born again. Then if we confess and accept Him, we are forgiven. Jesus is waiting for you.

Read the Following:

- Romans 3:23- "For we are all sinners…"
- Romans 6:23- "For the wage of sin is death…"
- John 3:3- "Unless someone is born again, he cannot see the Kingdom of God"
- John 14:6- Jesus said, "I am the way…"
- Romans 10:9-11- "If you confess…you will be saved…"
- 2 Corinthians 5:15- "And He died for all…"
- Revelation 3:20- "I stand at the door and knock…"

Pray:

> Father God, I am a sinner and I need forgiveness. I believe that Jesus died for me. I ask that you send the Holy Spirit into my life to guide me towards you. I earnestly seek to follow you all the days of my life. I give you my life, so I can live according to your will. Thank you for loving me and never leaving me. I ask this in Jesus' most precious name. - Amen

Congratulations on accepting the Lord! These are not merely words, they require action. Apply Jesus' teaching to your daily life and watch your transformation take place.

> Glory be to God!

Want to learn more? Sign-up for the Peace on Purpose online mini-course that coordinates with this book. This course will explore in depth how to apply scripture in daily situations to calm the chaos in your life. Visit the link below to find out more.

https://jennifer-s-school-db74.thinkific.com/

www.ingramcontent.com/pod-product-compliance
Lightning Source LLC
Chambersburg PA
CBHW071008080526
44587CB00015B/2389